CHRISTMAS IS . . .

Brentwood, Tennessee

Christmas Is . . .

ISBN 1-59475-046-7
Copyright © 2004 by GRQ, Inc.
Published by Blue Sky Ink, Brentwood, Tennessee.

Scripture quotations marked CEV are from the Contemporary English Version. Copyright © 1991, 1992, 1995 by American Bible Society. Used by permission.

Scripture quotations marked GNT are from the Good News Translation, Second Edition, Copyright © 1992 by American Bible Society. Used by permission. All rights reserved.

Scripture quotations marked KJV are from the King James Version of the Bible.

Scripture quotations marked THE MESSAGE are taken from THE MESSAGE. Copyright © by Eugene H. Peterson, 1993, 1994, 1995. Used by permission of NavPress Publishing Group.

Scripture quotations marked NASB are taken from the New American Standard Bible. Copyright © The Lockman Foundation 1960, 1962, 1963, 1968, 1971, 1972, 1973, 1975, 1977, 1995. Used by permission.

Scripture quotations marked NIV are taken from the Holy Bible, New International Version®. NIV®. Copyright © 1973, 1978, 1984 by International Bible Society. Used by permission of Zondervan Publishing House. All rights reserved.

Scripture quotations marked NKJV are taken from The New King James Version. Copyright © 1979, 1980, 1982, Thomas Nelson, Inc.

Scripture quotations marked NLT are taken from the Holy Bible, New Living Translation, copyright © 1996. Used by permission of Tyndale House Publishers, Inc., Wheaton, Illinois 60189. All rights reserved.

Scripture quotations marked NRSV are from the New Revised Standard Version of the Bible, copyright © 1989, 1997 by The Division of Christian Education of the National Council of the Churches of Christ in the USA. Used by permission. All rights reserved.

Editor: Lila Empson
Writer: Phillip H. Barnhart
Cover and Text Designer: Whisner Design Group

04 05 06   4 3 2 1

"The day will come," says the LORD,
"when I will make a new covenant
with the people of Israel and Judah."
Jeremiah 31:31 NLT

Contents

Introduction

Christmas is God deep in the flesh.
Martin Luther

෧෨

Christmas is God's love coming to everyone in Jesus Christ. Christmas is God putting his arms of deep and far reaching love around the world and hugging it to himself. Christmas is a cascade of ocean waves energizing your life. Christmas is a symphonic crescendo that plays and sings its way into your heart. Christmas is your best time of the year because it is a celebration of God's moving into your town, your neighborhood, your home, and into you.

Christmas is God in the flesh, making tangible God's feelings about you. You acknowledge such love when you put up your tree, decorate it with colors and shapes, and light it in joyful anticipation. You honor such a gift when you choose particular presents for special people and give them in love and appreciation. You affirm the coming of God in Christ when you read the story, sing the songs, listen to the Word, accept the truth, and feel the touch.

Christmas is knowing God loves you and comes to be with you. Christmas is God in your heart.

A child is born to us, a son is given to us.
Isaiah 9:6 NLT

• • • • • • • •

Just Like You

*When the fullness of time had come, God sent
his Son, born of a woman, born under the law.*

Galatians 4:4 NRSV

About a week before Christmas, five-year-old
Michael was busy with paints and brushes at his small
table. His mother came into the room and asked what he
was painting.

Michael pointed to paper stretched out on the table
and explained his picture, pointing to a brown structure
in the right corner of the paper. "This is baby Jesus'
house." Then, putting his finger on a large yellow star
above the house, he explained that the Wise Men found
the manger by looking at the star.

"And is that a Wise Man bringing gifts to Jesus?"
His mother pointed to a man carrying two bundles under
his arms.

"Oh no," Michael corrected his mother. "That's
Joseph taking out the trash."

. . . .

The whole Christmas story has an everyday feel to it. A man and a woman with a baby, trying to make do with what they had in circumstances beyond their control. Bad weather to contend with, noisy animals all around, trash to take out. The Christmas story is about real people contending with real life. It is about desire, struggle, and courage. It is about life with the lid off. It is about you.

When you see reality as the place God resides, facing reality brings assurance and satisfaction. Knowing that God is with you in all things is a gift of the Christian faith.

> Dear God, wherever I am and however I feel, you are with me. Thank you.
> ᴄᴏ⁓Amen.

• • • • • • • •

Light on the Subject

*His lamp shone over my head, and by
his light I walked through darkness.*

Job 29:3 NRSV

In a darkened laboratory in 1895, Wilhelm Roentgen got the surprise of his life. He rigged an induction coil and a mercury circuit breaker to a vacuum tube. When he switched on the current, to his amazement, a tray of barium crystals on a nearby bench began to glow. He then placed a sheet of lead between the crystals, and the tube and the crystals darkened. When he reached to remove the lead, to his increased amazement, his hand appeared in skeleton form. Unable to account for this phenomenon, he called the causative factor x-ray.

An x-ray makes light where no light is expected. It penetrates and uncovers things that are normally hidden. It shows what usually can't be seen.

Christmas is the birth date of Jesus Christ, the Light of the World. The light of Jesus uncovers who you

• • • • • • • •

are created to be. It shows your true and authentic nature. It reveals your heart of love. The light of Jesus puts you in touch with a greater virtue, and moves you to gratitude and generosity. It focuses on God's purpose for you, and it unfolds God's plan for you. It gives you a cadence of affirmation by which to march confidently forward in life.

You are more loving, more generous, more giving, and more forgiving when you stand in the light of Jesus.

> Dear God, bring the light
> you are to the life I live.
> Brighten my days and
> guard my nights.
>
> ∞Amen.

CHRISTMAS IS . . .

• • • • • • • •

🌿 The Christmas Story

The Lord himself will give you a sign:
The virgin will be with child and will give birth
to a son, and will call him Immanuel.

Isaiah 7:14 NIV

In the sixth month the angel Gabriel was sent by God to a
town in Galilee called Nazareth, to a virgin engaged to a man
whose name was Joseph, of the house of David. The virgin's
name was Mary. And he came to her and said, "Greetings,
favored one! The Lord is with you."

Luke 1:26–28 NRSV

"I am the Lord's servant," said Mary; "may it happen
to me as you have said." And the angel left her.

Luke 1:38 GNT

She cried out with a loud voice and said, "Blessed are you
among women, and blessed is the fruit of your womb!"

Luke 1:42 NASB

They entered the house where the child and his mother,
Mary, were, and they fell down before him and worshiped him.

Matthew 2:11 NLT

∽

16

• • • • • • • •

The Gift of Christmas 🎄

Christmas is God deep in the flesh.

Martin Luther

✍

God dances amidst the common.
And that night he did a waltz.

Max Lucado

✍

Christmas is not a date. It is a state of mind.

Mary Ellen Chase

✍

Love is what's in the room with
you at Christmas if you stop opening
presents and listen.

Eight-year-old girl

✍

To believe that the spirit of Christmas
does change lives and to labor for the
realization of it coming to all people
is the essence of our faith in Christ.

William Parks

✍

• • • • • • • •

Christmas Is Everywhere

Where could I go to escape from your
Spirit or from your sight?
Psalm 139:7 CEV

෨

At Christmastime, a family was driving around looking at manger scenes erected by various churches in their town. When they drove by the manger scene at one church, the precocious little one wanted to know who the figures represented. Dad pointed out Jesus, Mary, and Joseph.

They drove on and came to another church that had a Nativity scene set up and the same inquisitive one, upon seeing three figures with crowns on their heads, wanted to know who they were. Mom did the duties this time, explaining that the figures were the three Wise Men looking for the baby Jesus.

"Well, they won't find him there," the child said. "He's down at that other church."

The love of God that came down in Jesus Christ at

• • • • • • • •

Christmastime is not confined to church, tradition, or doctrine. God's love at Bethlehem is so great that it cannot be contained by your thoughts or circumscribed by your assumptions. It tears down any fences of preconception, theory, or creed you might have. It breaks through every limitation and speaks of the passion and esteem God has for everyone. Christmas lets God out of the box to invade the world with truth and presence.

Christmas knows where you are. It will find you and have its way with you.

Dear God, I am open to your presence in my life. Come and dwell in me.

ᴗ~Amen.

• • • • • • •

Make Room

She gave birth to her first-born son. She dressed
him in baby clothes and laid him on a bed of hay,
because there was no room for them in the inn.

Luke 2:7 CEV

ᐤ

They read the Christmas story a lot in Tracey's
house, and she had heard it many times. It was a good
story. There was a part of it Tracey didn't like, though,
and one Christmas she decided to do something about
that. So she asked her mom if she could read the
Christmas story this year instead of her mom or dad. Her
mom agreed that Tracey could indeed read the story.

When Christmas Eve came, everyone gathered in
the den. Tracey put the big family Bible on her small lap
and opened it to the appropriate place. When she came to
the place in the story where Joseph knocked on the
innkeeper's door, she read it like this: "Good evening, sir,
my wife is going to have a baby tonight. We need a place
to stay. Do you have room for us here?" The innkeeper,
according to Tracey, replied, "Well, our place is crowded,

20

• • • • • • • •

but there's always room for one more. Come on in."
Tracey closed the Bible on her lap, looked up at her family, and said gleefully, "Now, that's better, isn't it?"

It is better when there is room in your heart for the
Christ child of Bethlehem. It is better when you answer
the door as God knocks on it at Christmas, and let him
into your life.

> Dear God, I listen and
> hear you knock on the
> door of my heart. I
> make room for you
> in my life.
> ᏠᏰᎦᎻᎾ Amen.

CHRISTMAS IS . . .

* * * * * * * *

The Nativity

The Nativity scene originated with Saint Francis
of Assisi in 1224 in the little town of Greccio, Italy.
During his time, there were only a few books; but even
had there been more, most people could not read. Church
services were conducted in Latin, and Christmas held little meaning for most people. This worried Saint Francis
because he wanted to make the truth of Christmas clear
to everyone. No one should miss such a story, he rea-
soned. It is said that the good saint saw some shepherds
out in the fields near where he lived, and this inspired
him to depict the coming of Jesus in a way all could
understand. Before making his plans, he went to Rome to
discuss with the pope the idea of setting up a live Nativity
scene. After the pope gave his consent and blessing, the
saint asked a wealthy nobleman he knew well to help him

• • • • • • • •

prepare the presentation. Before Christmas came, news
spread rapidly. Crowds of worshipers, many with presents
for the holy baby, thronged to see this unusual way of
teaching the sacred story. The nobleman had assembled a
manger, some straw, a live ox, and a live donkey. Real
people took the parts of Mary, Joseph, and the shepherds.
Saint Francis himself arranged the scene, and reverently
placed a life-size figure of the Christ child in the manger.

. . . .

Into the Valley

Once upon a time, in a faraway land, lived a king who had power over all peoples. His courts were of the richest splendor, his tables heavy with the finest food, his castle filled with beautiful treasures from all over the world. The greatest musicians, poets, and philosophers were at his beck and call. Laughter and gaiety descended from his lofty castle. Clouds wrapped it in majesty as the sun danced all around in a ballet of wonder and grace. It seemed no darkness ever came to the castle. Those in the valley stopped to gaze at the castle and wished they could visit it, but no one was ever able to reach its pinnacle.

> The true light, which enlightens everyone, was coming into the world.
>
> John 1:9 NRSV

Once, in the cold of a gray winter, the king's favorite tailor entered the royal chambers with his latest

24

• • • • • • • •

samples of garments made from the finest fabrics. The tailor was proud of the materials he had chosen and of his past accomplishments in providing the king clothes for every occasion. He had woven these particular materials into the most wonderful clothes eyes had ever seen. They glistened like water and glittered like gold.

But the king was not pleased. He had not been pleased with much of anything for quite some time. His advisers found him restless, his friends saw in him little joy, and his family had no idea what was wrong with him. Nothing satisfied him, and the tailor's new creations proved no exception.

He ordered the tailor out of his chambers, vowing to make his own clothes. The door to the throne room was shut and locked, and the king stayed there for days. From inside the room came the clacking sound of a loom, and only those servants who brought his meals were allowed to see the king. The royal court waited with anticipation to see what the king would make for himself. They would surely be blinded by the glory of it.

The long-awaited day arrived. The door to the

• • • • • • • •

throne room opened, and the king emerged. Everyone, especially the tailor, gasped in shock and horror. The king was not dressed in majestic robes of bright colors. No satin or silk adorned his body. Instead, he was dressed in simple, inexpensive, and unlikely garments. They were plain of fabric and dull of color. As the king, he had the choice of the finest materials but had chosen instead to wear the clothes of a peasant. He did not look regal; he looked common. He did not look like a king; he looked like the subject of a king. Finally he announced that he was going down into the valley.

Down into the valley he went. Down to where the people he ruled lived. He went to their homes and to their jobs. He lived in their houses and worked alongside them in their fields. He laughed with them, cried with them, and couldn't get enough of being with them. He had never seen any of them before, and now he was with them all the time. He held their babies when they were born, went to the cemetery when they buried their fathers, and danced at the weddings of their daughters. He sat with them when they were sick and rejoiced with

• • • • • • • •

them when they were well. He celebrated their victories and lamented their defeats. He bragged on their successes and sympathized with their failures. He went where they went, ate what they ate, wore what they wore. He was, in every way, one of them.

This story about the king is something like what happened at Christmas. At Christmas, God visited the earth. He who was rich became poor. He who had glorious raiment dressed in common garments. He left the celestial palace and went down into the valley.

When humankind could not get to God, he came down. He put his arms around the world and hugged it to himself. Christmas is God spelling himself out in a language everybody can understand. At the heart of Christmas is a celebration of the incarnation of God in Jesus Christ. God became first an embryo, next a fetus, and then was born an infant among us. The Creator entered creation as a creature. God became approachable, accessible, touchable. God became a visible and tangible presence. God became flesh and blood. God came into the valley where you live. God moved into your neighborhood.

. . . .

The Christmas Story

A child is born to us, a son is given to us.

Isaiah 9:6 NLT

I will tell of the decree of the LORD: He said to me,
"You are my son; today I have begotten you."

Psalm 2:7 NRSV

His mother Mary was engaged to Joseph, but before
they were married, she found out that she was going
to have a baby by the Holy Spirit.

Matthew 1:18 GNT

An angel of the Lord appeared to him in a dream and
said, "Joseph son of David, do not be afraid to take
Mary home as your wife, because what is conceived
in her is from the Holy Spirit."

Matthew 1:20 NIV

When Joseph woke up, he did what the angel
of the Lord had commanded him and took
Mary home as his wife.

Matthew 1:24 NIV

• • • • • • • •

The Gift of Christmas 🌿

If anything were too good to
be true, Christmas would be.

Author Unknown

∽

The message of Christmas is that we
should never give up on God.

John L. Wallace

∽

When we could not go to him,
he came to us.

Donald Watson

∽

Your hands, so tiny, so tender, so white—
clutched tonight in an infant's fist.

Max Lucado

∽

The truth of Christmas is that the
child of Christmas is God.

John F. MacArthur

∽

• • • • • • • •

A Real Baby

Overcome, they kneeled and worshiped him. Then they opened their luggage and presented gifts: gold, frankincense, myrrh.

Matthew 2:11 THE MESSAGE

ରୁ

In preparation for Christmas, a Sunday school teacher asked her children to write on small slips of paper the kind of gift the infant Jesus would like and could use. They were to drop the slips into a box near a manger scene set up in the classroom. Some of the children misunderstood and, instead of the name of a gift, they put the gift itself. In the box, the teacher found a jar of baby food, a small teddy bear, a toy truck, a tiny pair of mittens, and a disposable diaper. At their classroom party, the children were to "show and tell" their gifts. The little girl who had given the disposable diaper explained that Jesus was a real baby and that real babies need diapers.

Christmas is God becoming a real baby. Jesus sometimes slept quietly in his crib, and other times he twisted restlessly. He smiled, cried, got hungry, and needed his

· · · · · · ·

diapers changed. Incarnation may be a big word, but it means simply that God took on human form. God became touchable, squeezable, pinchable, and holdable. Jesus was pleasant and irritable, had good days and bad days, brought to those around him both joy and concern. God became all the way human. Christmas is a real story with a real baby.

God's love came from heaven to earth to enter your heart. The truth of Christmas is real for you.

> Thank you, God, for being real. I am grateful for your touch on my life.
> ☙Amen.

• • • • • • • •

The King Is Coming

*They asked around, "Where can we find and pay
homage to the newborn King of the Jews?"*
Matthew 2:2 THE MESSAGE

∽

When the president of the United States visits a
city or a town, much preparation is made. "The president
is coming!" gets people in high gear and sends them scur-
rying. Committees are formed and assignments made.
Dignitaries write speeches, and bands rehearse musical
numbers. Streets are cleaned and buildings painted.
Schoolchildren do projects. Banners and flags spring up
everywhere. Nothing is left undone for the president's
visit.

"The King is coming!" this Christmas. You prepare
for his coming by making room in your heart for him.
That is the place he wants to be. Jesus Christ is most at
home as King when he rules from a heart-shaped throne
at the center of your life. He wants to sit there every day
and help you make decisions about your life. He wants to

• • • • • • • •

be the Sovereign of your thoughts, attitudes, and actions.
He wants to be the Monarch of your job, your family, and
your every minute. He wants to be the King of all you are
and are becoming.

You can have God in your heart. You can worship
God in your heart. You can love God with your heart.
You can give God your heart, the best gift he ever gets.

This Christmas, fill your heart with Jesus.
It will be bigger and better than ever.

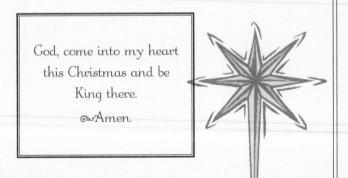

God, come into my heart
this Christmas and be
King there.
ᴔAmen.

• • • • • • • •

The Christmas Story

A star shall come out of Jacob, and a scepter
shall rise out of Israel.

Numbers 24:17 NRSV

You, O Bethlehem Ephrathah, are only a small village
in Judah. Yet a ruler of Israel will come from you.

Micah 5:2 NLT

I will establish the throne of his kingdom forever.

2 Samuel 7:13 NRSV

See, I lay a stone in Zion, a tested stone, a
precious cornerstone for a sure foundation.

Isaiah 28:16 NIV

You are blessed by God above all other women,
and your child is blessed. . . . You are blessed, because
you believed that the Lord would do what he said.

Luke 1:42, 45 NLT

• • • • • • •

The Gift of Christmas

We can give the world Christ. We cannot give
it more, and we dare not give it less.

William Temple

❧

Our main job is not to cry "Look what the
world has come to" but "Look who has
come to the world."

Kermit L. Long

❧

When I say God, I think Jesus.

E. Stanley Jones

❧

My nomination for history's most profound
event is the incarnation of God in Christ.

Ralph Bailey

❧

Jesus Christ is the centerpiece of
the masterpiece.

Kathryn Ingram

❧

. . . .

Christmas Presence

In Your presence is fullness of joy; at Your
right hand are pleasures forevermore.
Psalm 16:11 NKJV

꙳

A few days before Christmas, Weyland was at the
shopping mall buying presents for the twenty-three
employees at the meat-packing plant he owned and oper-
ated. He bought fancy pen sets for his secretary and his
manager. An electronic dictionary for the delivery boy
who went to college part-time. Leather address books for
his accountant and the personnel manager. Weyland pur-
chased other items until he had something for everyone.

Not a good gift-wrapper, Weyland had all the presents wrapped at the mall and loaded them high in the
backseat of his car. He would give each person a gift the
following morning when everybody was at work. Driving
home, he passed several churches with various messages
and slogans posted on outside marquees. With all the
presents in the backseat piled almost to the roof of his car,

• • • • • • • •

one of the signs particularly caught his attention. It said, THINKING OF CHRISTMAS PRESENCE?

The greatest message of Christmas is that of God's presence. God in Jesus Christ is with you. He is with you everywhere all the time. He never takes a vacation or a long weekend. Christmas is God coming boldly into your life and staying there as your everyday companion. Wherever you walk, God walks beside you. Whatever you pass through, God passes through it with you.

God comes to you and draws you to himself.

37

God, you are 24/7,
on duty in my life
all the time
☙Amen.

• • • • • • • •

Joy Requires It

*You bestow on him blessings forever; you make
him glad with the joy of your presence.*

Psalm 21:6 NRSV

෨

In *Burning Bright* by John Steinbeck, Joe Saul
longs for a baby. When his wife tells him she is pregnant,
he dances for joy. He tells a close friend he wants to buy
his wife a wonderful present that will delight and please
her. He describes this desire as a compulsion. It is something he has to do. There is no option. Trying to explain
his feeling to a friend, he says, "My joy requires a symbol."

The gift of God in Jesus Christ brings you great joy.
The joy of knowing you are loved beyond measure and
valued beyond compare. The joy of believing God's Son
stepped across the threshold of heaven, walked over the
stars, and came to earth to be with you. The joy of claim-
ing the gift of God in Jesus Christ is personally yours. It is
a joy that creates cause for celebration everywhere and all
the time. It is a joy that grabs hold of you, won't let you
go, and insists on a response.

• • • • • • • •

Someone asked Joseph Haydn, the famous composer, why his music was so bright and cheerful. He replied, "I cannot make it otherwise. When I think upon God, my heart is so full of joy that the notes dance and leap from my pen."

The joy of God that came to earth at Christmas requires your response.

Dear God, my heart
jumps with the joy of
your love for me.
∽Amen.

The Story of the Candy Cane

The tradition of Christmas candy canes began in the Middle Ages when mothers wanted to calm their fidgety babies during long church services. The mothers invented pacifiers for their babies made out of white sugar sticks. Sometime in the seventeenth century, a choir leader in Germany noticed how effective the sugar sticks were and appropriated them for his own use with an interesting modification. He bent the straight sticks into cane shapes to symbolize the staffs of the shepherds who heard the good news about Jesus on a Bethlehem hillside from an angelic chorus. The choir leader gave the shepherd staff sticks, as a holiday treat, to children who sang in his choir. The new shape of the canes helped the children remember the first visitors to the manger, and also reminded them about whom they were singing. Some of

• • • • • • • •

the older children noticed that when you turned the cane upside down, it made the letter J—for Jesus.

Over the years, the Christmas candy cane became a favorite throughout Europe and then in America. Someone added red stripes to indicate that Jesus was God's gift of love and forgiveness and, later, someone put a fresh peppermint taste into the candy to symbolize that lives are made pure and sweet by God's gift of grace in Jesus Christ.

• • • • • • • •

What Christmas Does

In December 1944, during World War II, American soldiers were stationed at the edge of Germany in Hurtgen Forest, anticipating what history records as the Battle of the Bulge. A heavy winter snow blanketed the forest and made any substantial movement on the part of the soldiers difficult. A few days before Christmas, about twilight, a group of soldiers was slowly driving through the countryside when they noticed about twenty–five German civilians, all dressed in black, trudging deliberately up the road. The civilians had to step into the deep snowbanks to let the military vehicles pass, and some of them fell down.

One of the soldiers, let's call him Farley Jones, became vividly aware of how negative he felt about the

> I will both lie down in peace, and sleep; for You alone, O LORD, make me dwell in safety.
>
> Psalm 4:8 NKJV

42

• • • • • • • •

German people as he watched the civilians along the road. For one thing, he was suspicious. How could he tell what their actual intentions were? They might be hiding enemy soldiers in their homes, or have some of them stashed along the road. Anyway, if it were not for the Germans, he would be home getting ready to celebrate Christmas with his wife and three children.

As the military vehicles moved slowly toward a crossroad, a small, white frame church became visible to Farley. The civilians were headed in its direction. They were going to church. It dawned on Farley that it was Christmas Eve and, had he been home, he, too, would have been going to church. This thought accelerated his resentment. Here these German men were, with their wives and children, and he was all alone. He was cold, miserable, and fighting in a terrible war.

Up ahead of Farley and the American troops was another group of German civilians entering the church they had seen. As the civilians opened the door and went into the church, a warm light made its way into the cold darkness. Farley could see the soft glow of lighted candles

43

. . . .

in the windows of the church. A few more people went into the church and kept the door open long enough for Farley to see beautiful stained-glass windows and a white-robed pastor standing under one of them. The church was already nearly full. The first group of people he had seen arrived at the church door and went in, and the Christmas Eve service began.

The military vehicles had come to a halt. A late-comer arrived and, as the door opened, the American soldiers heard the people singing. The sound of reverent voices wafted over the landscape, singing "Stille Nacht." Farley had known that carol from his childhood and, before realizing it, he added his English to their German and joined them in singing about that great night when God came to earth in Jesus Christ. As he walked by the church and the music of the congregation faded, Farley continued singing as the soldiers plodded down the treacherous road.

The next day, when the troops had found a place to make camp, Farley Jones went to see the chaplain. It was Christmas Day. He had not slept the night before. "Silent

• • • • • • • •

Night" kept singing its tune in his mind. Its words of
wonder, glory, and joy rolled over and over in Farley's
heart. Especially, its sentiment of calm and peace spoke to
him. He needed calm and peace in the midst of disruption
and war. He needed to be at peace with others, with the
German civilians on the road. He needed to be at peace
with himself. This is what he told the chaplain, and they
spent a long time together talking about the tragedy of
war and God's love for all people and how peace is what
God sent Jesus Christ to earth to bring. That day, Farley
Jones dedicated himself to peace.

45

When the war was over and Farley was back home
with his wife and children, he worked hard in the family
insurance business as he had before the war. But now he
approached everything differently. He perceived every
client as someone God loved. He was also a more devoted
husband, a better father, a more grateful son. Nothing
was the same for Farley after the night he passed by that
small, white frame church in the Hurtgen Forest of
Germany and heard God's people singing about God's
Son. 🍂

· · · · · · · · ·

The Christmas Story

A shoot will come up from the stump of Jesse;
from his roots a Branch will bear fruit.

Isaiah 11:1 NIV

Because Joseph was a descendant of King David, he had
to go to Bethlehem in Judea, David's ancient home.

Luke 2:4 NLT

While they were there, the time came for her
to deliver her child.

Luke 2:6 NRSV

All this took place to fulfill what was spoken
by the Lord through the prophet.

Matthew 1:22 NASB

She gave birth to her firstborn son and wrapped
in bands of cloth, and laid him in a manger.

Luke 2:7 NRSV

. . . .

The Gift of Christmas

He became the Son of Man so that we might
become the sons and daughters of God.

Lorine Finch

෨ඏ

Gifts seem to be what Christmas is all about.

Donna W. Payne

෨ඏ

Jesus Christ is the absolute union
between the divine and the human.

William R. Cannon

෨ඏ

Jesus is God's love in person on earth.

Phil Muth

෨ඏ

The Lord was as much God as if he
were not man at all and as much man
as if he were not God at all.

Jess Moody

෨ඏ

• • • • • • • •

Christ Is Coming

He came to his own people, but they didn't want
him. But whoever did want him, who believed he
was who he claimed and would do what he said,
he made to be their true selves.

John 1:11–12 THE MESSAGE

☙

The countdown to Christmas is on. You look in the newspaper and see how many days you have left until Christmas. Your personal calendar marks the turning of daily pages toward the big day. "Christmas is coming!" Anticipation accelerates and expectation reigns. Closets hide presents. Children make lists and write letters. Parents plot and plan. "Christmas is coming!" Churches rehearse and stage. Communities decorate; businesses get ready. "Christmas is coming!" People make travel plans; students look forward to time off. Charities gear up to help others. "Christmas is coming!"

A different sort of announcement helps you get ready for the heart of Christmas. It calls you to the purity of Christmas, its foundational truth. "Christ is coming!" This announcement invites you to a revelation of hope

. . . .

and a declaration of love. It reduces the accumulative layers of the season to a core of meaning and significance. It defines Christmas. It makes the definitive statement about Christmas. "Christ is coming!" When you understand this statement, you get ready to go to Bethlehem. You anticipate standing in front of the manger and knowing who is in it. You prepare to move from the circumference of Christmas to stand at its center. "Christ is coming."

Christ is coming to you this Christmas. Your gift is visitation. Your present is presence.

49

Dear God, I sense your purpose
and feel your love as you make
your way to my heart.
∾Amen.

• • • • • • • •

Up In Arms

*He took them up in his arms,
laid his hands on them, and blessed them.*

Mark 10:16 NRSV

⤾

A beautiful and beloved world dignitary visited a large city in the United States and insisted that a trip to a hospital with a special ward for children be included in her itinerary. She wanted to visit the ward that held children who had been born to AIDS victims. These children were infected and destined to die young. In the children's ward, the beautiful and beloved woman went from bed to bed visiting the victims and sharing with them her elegance, charm, and love. At one point, and without anyone's approval, she picked up a little boy, held him in her arms, and whispered something special enough in his ear to put a large smile on his face.

Christmas is God picking up the world, putting the arms of Christ around it, and hugging it to himself. It is the embrace of hope, the touch of truth, the whisper of

• • • • • • • •

love. It is God holding you in a place where you feel
alone. It is God coming to you at a time when you didn't
think anyone would show up. Christmas is the sweet
assurance that God keeps company with you on a daily
basis and that his presence has import and substance.
Christmas puts a smile on your face and a song in
your heart.

Christmas comes to you wherever you are
and embraces you as you are.

Dear God, thank you for
lifting and loving me.
Thank you for holding
and hugging me.
᧞Amen.

• • • • • • • •

The Christmas Story

All nations will be blessed through him,
and they will call him blessed.

Psalm 72:17 NIV

Jesus was born in the town of Bethlehem in Judea,
during the reign of King Herod.

Matthew 2:1 NLT

We saw his star in the east and have
come to worship him.

Matthew 2:2 CEV

The star, which they had seen in the east,
went on before them until it came and stood
over the place where the Child was.

Matthew 2:9 NASB

When they saw the star, they rejoiced
with exceedingly great joy.

Matthew 2:10 NKJV

• • • • • • • •

The Gift of Christmas 🍂

I know that God is love,
because Christ is love.

Martin Luther King Jr.

૭૨

The incarnation is the affirmation
of God's faith in his creation.

Reuel L. Howe

૭૨

God is engaged in the world
without ceasing to be God.

Thomas C. Odden

૭૨

Jesus was a perfect man perfectly
filled with the Holy Spirit.

Clovis G. Chappell

૭૨

Jesus comes into the world where
God is unapproachable and reverses
our main concept of God.

H. S. Vigeveno

૭૨

• • • • • • • •

He Is God

The Word . . . was with God, and he was God.

John 1:1 NLT

෨

A class of first graders in a church school was asked by their teacher to write their version of the nativity story. They took the assignment seriously and got to work on the production. There was a familiar cast: Joseph, Mary, shepherds, Wise Men, and animals of various styles and sizes. There was also an angel propped up in the background. But everything else was modernized. There was some sort of makeshift partition, behind which Mary was apparently in labor. She groaned loudly, and other voices could be heard giving her encouragement. Suddenly, the "doctor" emerged from the "delivery room" in a white coat wearing a visor and stethoscope. He ran over to one of the children standing there, slapped him solidly on the back, and gleefully announced, "Congratulations, Joseph, it's a God!"

• • • • • • • •

As you get to the Christmas story this year, make no mistake about it. That is God in the manger. The sweet little baby, romantically embraced across the years, is a divine person in human form. He is as fully God as he is fully human. Jesus is God with skin on, a tangible and touchable presence. He fills the space between God and you with himself. He brings God to you, and you to God.

Christmas is about the deity of Jesus. God was born into the world.

55

God, thank you for opening heaven's window and showing me what you are like.

∞Amen.

CHRISTMAS IS . . .

• • • • • • • •

The Story of the Christmas Tree

 After Martin Luther married and had a family, one Christmas Eve he was walking home through the forest and was deeply impressed by the myriad stars in the winter sky, and also by the beauty of the stately evergreens. When Luther reached home, he tried to explain the glory of the scene to his wife and children, but words failed him. So he went out, cut down a small fir, and placed lighted candles on it to represent the starry sky over the stable the night Christ was born. This custom, initiated to teach the Christmas story, eventually spread everywhere.

In the United States, the first decorated Christmas trees are said to have been the ones set up during the American Revolution by homesick Hessian soldiers hired by King George III to fight the rebellious colonists. The

. . . .

first Christmas tree in a home in the United States was
put up by Charles Follen, a German professor at Harvard.
During the 1850s, while he was president of the country,
Franklin Pierce and his wife entertained the entire
Sunday school of the New York Presbyterian Church with
a Christmas tree. In 1891, President Benjamin Harrison
had a Christmas tree put in the White House, and played
Santa Claus for his grandchildren. He expressed the wish
that all families would follow his example.

• • • • • • •

Angels Singing

Rudy had recently learned his company was transferring him to a different location. He, his wife, and Sally, their five-year-old daughter, would have to move all the way across the country. The move would especially affect Sally, who had a houseful of friends all the time and whose grandparents lived only three miles away. It would not be easy for her. Rudy and his wife, Nora, had put off telling her. Besides, it was Christmastime, and Sally was all excited about her part as an angel in the big play at church.

> Suddenly, the angel was joined by a vast host of others—the armies of heaven—praising God.
>
> Luke 2:13 NLT
>
> ೮ಎ

Sally was precious, with her ringlet hair and a personality to match. She was also bright as a bulb and sensed something was going on with her mom and dad. Whatever it was, she wanted to help them. When they seemed sad, she tried to cheer them up by being funny.

58

• • • • • • • •

When Rudy and Nora were talking together and looked
so serious, she interrupted by telling them she needed or
wanted something.

As Christmas approached, Sally was busy practicing
her part as an angel in the church play. Her mom made
her outfit out of scraps in her sewing room, and her dad
made a wand out of something he had in his workshop.
The angel outfit was all white and shiny. The wand
gleamed silver and had a star at its top. Sally was proud of
her costume.

They all went to church together that Christmas
Eve, and Sally was superb in her role as the angel who
told the shepherds about Jesus. She spoke clearly and joyfully the heavenly announcement, "I bring you good news
of great joy." Her dad and mom beamed with pride. Nora
winked at her, and Rudy gave her a thumbs-up. Seeing
their affirmation, Sally glowed even more radiantly.

When Rudy, Nora, and Sally got home they sat
down in the living room for a traditional Christmas Eve
experience. Each one of them got to choose one present to
open. The presents had been arranged under the tree in
such a way that the big-time ones were saved until

CHRISTMAS IS . . .

. . . .

Christmas morning. Rudy got a new wallet, Nora a cutting board for the kitchen, and Sally a doll that was all soft and cuddly and giggled when Sally squeezed her.

Rudy and Nora had planned to tell Sally about their move across the country and try to deal with her feelings of loss, but they just couldn't bring themselves to do it yet. They agreed to do it the day after Christmas. At one point, right after she got her doll, Sally sensed they were about to tell her something. But they didn't.

It was time to go to bed, and Sally held her doll in her arms as she walked up the steps. About halfway up, she stopped at a window and stood still there. "Go on to bed, honey," her mother said. Sally didn't move. Instead, she opened the window.

"What are you doing?" her father asked. "Close the window, darling," her mother added, "the house will get cold." Sally turned toward Nora and Rudy and, when she did, her face was glowing as it had during the play at church. She said, "I'm listening to the angels." Rudy and Nora walked hand in hand quickly up the steps. When they arrived, she repeated herself. "Oh, Daddy and Mommy, I'm listening to the angels sing." Rudy and Nora smiled at each other. Their daughter had always been

• • • • • • • •

spiritually sensitive. When she was a baby they had often stood over her crib and said the angels must be talking to her.

Now, this Christmas Eve, they were singing to her. Rudy and Nora didn't hear anything but had no doubt their daughter did. Rudy pulled Sally to him and gave her a big hug. As he did, the doll Sally held giggled, and they all had a good laugh. Nora put one arm around her husband and another around her daughter and said a prayer in her heart that, after a while, came onto her lips. "O God," she said, "thank you for our family. Thank you for this evening at the church. And thank you so much for our sweet, wonderful daughter who hears the angels sing."

Rudy said, "Amen."

Then, as she turned to go to bed, Sally added an addendum to the prayer. "Dear Jesus," she said, "let Mommy and Daddy know that whatever's been troubling them, everything's going to be all right."

All three of them opened their eyes at the same time, and Sally's parents gave her a puzzled look. Answering their look, she said, "That's what the angels sang to me tonight."

CHRISTMAS IS . . .

• • • • • • • •

❦The Christmas Story

Says the Lord GOD: I myself will take a sprig from the
lofty top of a cedar . . . I myself will plant it.

Ezekiel 17:22 NRSV

I have made a covenant with my chosen one,
I have sworn to David my servant,
"I will establish your line forever."

Psalm 89:3–4 NIV

I will cause a horn to sprout up for David;
I have prepared a lamp for my anointed one.

Psalm 132:17 NRSV

Where will the Messiah be born?

Matthew 2:4 GNT

In Bethlehem . . . for this is what the prophet wrote.

Matthew 2:5 NLT

࿂

. . . .

The Gift of Christmas

It was the greatest condescension the
world has ever known.

John F. MacArthur

෨

God could not stay apart from the evil
of the world and redeem it.

George Buttrick

෨

The doctrine of the incarnation is the
doctrine of the personalization of love.

Reuel L. Howe

෨

God did not cast His benefits down from the
door of heaven; He came down to earth with
His heart in them.

Warren W. Wiersbe

෨

Jesus seals the past, closes the period of
waiting, and becomes incarnate in history.

Carlo Carretto

෨

• • • • • • • •

Cradle and Cross

This is how much God loved the world: He gave
his Son, his one and only Son.

John 3:16 THE MESSAGE

တ

The Wise Men in T. S. Eliot's "Journey of the
Magi" finally make it to the manger after days of risk,
trial, and struggle. The path has been difficult and arduous. They nearly lost their lives as peril after peril plagued
their journey. Obstacles and obstructions have been many,
and they wondered many times if they would make it
under any circumstance. As they arrive at the manger it
seems there is a shadow of a cross over the cradle. They
ask, "Were we led all that way for Birth or Death?"

In the midst of all the sentiment and romance of the
Christmas story, keep in sight the fact that Jesus was born
to die. The end of this story is distant in tenor and timbre
from its beginning. The beginning is so sweet and tender,
the end so harsh and cruel. From a cradle to a cross. From
loved ones gathered around laughing and rejoicing to

• • • • • • • •

loved ones assembled in grief and sorrow. What began in anticipation and hope ended in regret and disappointment. That is exactly as it was supposed to be. The shadowy silhouette of a cruciform death hovering over the purity and innocence of a manger birth is precisely what God had in mind.

Jesus was born to die for you because you are worth dying for.

Dear Jesus, thank you for loving me
enough to give yourself up for me.
ஐAmen.

Your Gifts

They brought out their gifts of gold, frankincense,
and myrrh, and presented them to him.

Matthew 2:11 GNT

༄

During the Advent season, a leader of a women's
Bible study group asked the question: "Would it have
made any difference if three Wise Women instead of three
Wise Men had come to visit baby Jesus on that first
Christmas?" Another woman required no time to think
that over and immediately replied, "Absolutely! They
would have asked for directions, arrived on time, helped
deliver the baby, cleaned the stable, made a casserole, and
brought disposable diapers as gifts."

There is much you can do for God. You can seek his
will and walk in his way. You can spend time with God in
prayer, meditation, and worship. You can nurture your
inner life and then make your outer life an expression of
your inward dimension. You can help God's people. You
can find where hurt is and help God bring healing to it.

• • • • • • • •

You can identify sickness and help God give health and wholeness. You can affirm God's love for you, and give your love tangibly to others. You can get up each day, thank God for the next twenty-four hours, and seek to bring beauty and peace to each minute. You can tell the truth, be absolutely honest in all areas, and do what you say you will do. There is much you can do for God.

You are special to God. What you do for God is important to him.

Dear God, may I serve you in everything. Make my life one of service to you.

∽Amen.

· · · · · · · ·

The Christmas Story

The shepherds said to one another, "Let us go now to
Bethlehem and see this thing that has taken place."

Luke 2:15 NRSV

When they saw this, they made known what had been
told them about this child.

Luke 2:17 NRSV

All who heard it were amazed at what
the shepherds told them.

Luke 2:18 NRSV

Mary treasured all these words and pondered
them in her heart.

Luke 2:19 NRSV

The shepherds returned, glorifying and praising
God for all the things they had heard and seen.

Luke 2:20 NIV

ও

• • • • • • • •

The Gift of Christmas 🌿

Jesus was the Christ because he was the union
of spirit and matter, God in the flesh.

L. Robert Keck

֍

Jesus Christ was an infusion of
divine life into materiality.

Flannery O'Connor

֍

He is both great in the nature of God,
and small in the form of a servant.

Saint Augustine

֍

His birth was wonderful, for no
other ever occurred that was like it.

Elijah P. Brown

֍

He is majesty in the midst of the mundane.

Max Lucado

֍

• • • • • • • •

Embraced at Christmas

Live in peace; and the God of love
and peace will be with you.
2 Corinthians 13:11 NKJV

During World War I, guns of ally and enemy poured death upon helpless troops deep in the trenches of France. Death reigned on the hard throne of hate and revenge. Night came and the guns finally fell silent, but troops on both sides waited poised for more battle.

However, it was Christmas Eve, the time of miracles, and one occurred there. In the midst of that drama of fear and tragedy, there was heard coming from the German trenches the singing of Christmas carols. Overcome by contrast and the counterpoint of joy, the Allied troops joined the singing. They sang and sang in unparalleled harmony. Their voices blended and then amalgamated.

In the midst of the singing, first one side and then the other began moving out of the trenches. No

• • • • • • • •

agreement had been made, no command given. Spontaneously and freely, the two sides moved toward each other. The music continued, and as they met singing the age-old melodies of birth and life, they shook hands and embraced under a Christmas moon. That was the night God's will was done on earth as it is done in heaven.

When you embrace one another in love and peace, God's kingdom comes on earth and angels sing for joy.

71

I have looked for the way to peace, O God, and now I know that peace is the way.
୬Amen.

• • • • • • • •

A Different Way Home

Having been warned in a dream not to go
back to Herod, they returned to their country
by another route.

Matthew 2:12 NIV

☙

A woman from Maine was visiting some of her
family at Christmastime in a small town in the Deep
South. As she drove around one day, she was surprised to
find in the town square a crèche with the three Wise Men
wearing firefighter helmets. She stopped at a nearby
church and asked the secretary why that was so. She did
not recall reading anything about firefighters in the Bible
when Jesus was born. "You Yankees never read the
Bible!" the secretary said. She took out a Bible, flipped
through some pages, and pointed to a passage. "Look!"
she exclaimed. "It says right here that they came from
afar."

That is the way the story of the Magi begins, but
the way it ends is the best news for you this Christmas. It
says that after they saw the baby Jesus and worshiped him

• • • • • • •

with praise and gifts, they went home by a way different
from the way they had come. Of course, this was to avoid
Herod's wrath, but think of the implications of that idea.
When you make it to the manger and know who that is
in the manger, you have to go home a different way
because you are never again the same person.

Knowing God came to earth in Jesus Christ
makes you a new creation—which is possible all the
time and impossible none of the time.

73

> Dear God, this
> Christmas I look forward
> to being renewed and
> reignited. Thank you for
> the power of change.
> ∽Amen.

. . . .

The Story of the Poinsettia

A story is told of Pepita, a poor Mexican girl who had no gift to present to the Christ child at the Christmas Eve service. This made her sad as she trudged to the church with her cousin Pedro. "I am sure," he said, "that if you give the most humble gift in love, it is accepted by God." Pepita stopped on the road and gathered a handful of common weeds, forming them into a small bouquet before she entered the church. She remembered her cousin's words as she approached the altar. She surely offered her gift with the greatest of love for Christ. As she laid the bouquet on the altar at the base of the Nativity scene, the weeds suddenly burst into blossoms of brilliant red. From that day, the bright red flowers were known as Flores de Noche Buena, or Flowers of the Holy Night, and bloomed each year during the Christmas season.

• • • • • • • •

Franciscan priests near Taxco, Mexico, began using the flower in Nativity processions because of its brilliant color.

This beautiful flower was discovered by Dr. Joel Roberts Poinsett of Charleston, South Carolina, in the 1820s when he was the first ambassador from the United States to Mexico. He sent cuttings of it to a nurseryman in Philadelphia, who named it after the ambassador.

• • • • • • • •

In the Manger

Nate, his wife, Stella, and their two daughters had just returned from a Christmas Eve service. Nate had been greatly blessed by the singing and the sermon, but he was a little lonely as he made his way to the barn out back where he kept his cows. There had been an empty spot on their pew at the church, and a vacant place at the dinner table earlier that evening. Their nineteen-year-old son, Danny, was in Korea with the army. Nate missed him so much.

> What is born of the flesh is flesh, and what is born of the Spirit is spirit.
>
> John 3:6 NRSV

As Nate made his way across a long meadow and into the barn, he recalled the many times he and Danny had gone there together. Danny had always been his right-hand man. He particularly remembered one Christmas Eve when they went to the barn to check on a sick cow. Snow lay thick on the ground as they pulled coat collars up around their necks and stocking caps down over their ears. As cold as they were, Nate stopped

76

• • • • • • • •

to repair a gate that had been blown down in a storm. As always, Danny pitched in to help his dad. They were as close as any father and son. Arriving at the barn, they slid open a stubborn door and entered. It was much warmer inside, and Danny pulled off his stocking cap and stuck it in his hip pocket, his rusty hair falling down over his ears as he shook his head and laughed at his dad stomping the snow off his boots. "I bet Mom doesn't know you can dance like that," he teased Nate.

Nate went to a side stall to care for the sick cow, and Danny stood in the middle of the barn taking off his coat and dropping it on the floor. Fresh from hearing the Christmas story and singing the old familiar Christmas carols at church, Danny said later that he experienced the cow barn in a different way that night. He listened to the soft munching of the cows, smelled the hay, and took in the aroma of the animals. Light bulbs dangling from the ceiling on spindly wires cast long shadows that played and danced across the barn. The old family dog lay in a corner, and a cat skittered across the floor. He looked to the stall where his dad cared for the sick cow, and his father's silhouette formed a strong and stalwart caricature against the side of the wall.

CHRISTMAS IS . . .

. . . .

Danny walked to the stall, joined Nate there, put his hand on his shoulder, and said, "Look, Dad, we're in the manger."

His dad laughed and said, "What do you mean, son?" Danny explained, "Look around us, Dad. The animals, the hay, you and me in a barn. It's like being in Bethlehem, in the manger, with Joseph and Mary and Jesus. It's like we were whisked back there all those years ago. We're in the manger."

Nate turned from the cow, laid his arm on Danny's back, and said, "You're right, Danny, you're right. We are in the manger."

"That's where we are, all right," Danny added.

Nate remembered that night six years before as he checked on the cows and cleaned up a couple of stalls. Just then, Stella joined him in the barn. She had put the girls to bed and wanted to be with her husband. They were holding hands when the phone shrilled over the extension in the barn. They both jumped and looked anxious, as they had prayed in church that Danny would be able to get a call through to them from Korea. He had indicated in a letter that it might be possible. Nate picked up the phone. "Hello," he said worriedly.

78

• • • • • • • •

"Merry Christmas, Dad!" he heard Danny say in a clear and loud voice.

"Hello, son. We went to church this evening, and the girls are in bed. We're over in the barn."

There was a pause on the other end of the line and then Danny said, "Oh, Dad, you're in the manger, aren't you?"

Nate smiled across the miles. "That's exactly where we are. Mom and I are in the manger."

"So am I, Dad," Danny replied. "So am I."

The world is Jesus' manger. You are never away from Bethlehem. 🌿

• • • • • • • •

The Christmas Story

All peoples on earth will be blessed through you.

Genesis 12:3 NIV

All the prophets . . . from Samuel and those
after him, also predicted these days.

Acts 3:24 NRSV

I will preserve an heir for him; his throne will be
as endless as the days of heaven.

Psalm 89:29 NLT

The Word became flesh and blood,
and moved into the neighborhood.

John 1:14 THE MESSAGE

The law was given through Moses; grace
and truth came through Jesus Christ.

John 1:17 NIV

. . . .

The Gift of Christmas

God was in him as he was, and that was enough.

John Killinger

In the incarnation, God illuminated
the world by his wisdom and excited
it to the love of himself.

Peter Abelard

He was a man with one foot planted in
time and the other in eternity.

Terry Fullum

God entered into an ordinary home
and into an ordinary family.

William Barclay

By his incarnation, Jesus demonstrated that
our bodies are not inherently evil.

Charles and Virginia Sell

• • • • • • • •

Where Is He?

Where is the newborn king of the Jews?
We have seen his star as it arose,
and we have come to worship him.

Matthew 2:2 NLT

☙

Credentialed astrologers from the East, weary from months of travel, arrived in Bethlehem on a momentous night. The star they had diligently and faithfully followed had stopped and perched in a most unlikely place. It hovered in announcement over a cave cut by wind and storm into the side of a limestone hill. They had asked the provincial authority and his advisers the "where" question, and now they knew the answer. They sighed collectively among themselves. This was the hallowed spot. This was the holy place. This was the birthplace of the King.

There is an answer to your "where" question about God. You need not be in the dark about God's location because that is what the light of Christmas is about. The door that leads to God was opened once and for all on the

• • • • • • • •

night the Wise Men saw that the star had stopped over the cave. Because of that night, you know where God is.

God is in Christ. It is from that position he speaks to you this Christmas of how much he loves you. It is from that position he wants you to know how much you are worth. God loves you so much that he could not stay in heaven. God came to be with you because you are worth so much.

God doesn't see the person you see when you look in the mirror. God sees more clearly who you really are.

> Thank you, dear God, for loving me enough to come to me in a way I can understand.
>
> ⌒Amen.

• • • • • • • •

What Obedience Does

"I am the Lord's servant," said Mary; "may it
happen to me as you have said."
Luke 1:38 GNT

᭤

Mary's obedience to God is why there is a
Christmas. The go-ahead she gave God set the plan in
motion for Jesus to be born in Bethlehem. This simple
peasant girl could have responded in many ways to the
angel's announcement that she was going to be the mother of God's Son. She could have rejected what the angel
said. She could have thought that she was going crazy. Or
she could have rolled over and gone back to sleep. She did
none of that. She simply said yes and awaited further
instructions.

The key to great meaning in your life is a Mary-like
obedience to God. Obedience opens the door to the power
God has reserved for you and to the possibilities already
accumulating down the path of your future. Obedience
sets you free to step outside your will into God's will. In
God's will, you are in a larger place.

• • • • • • •

Oswald Chambers said, "Spiritual maturity is not reached by the passing of the years, but by obedience to the will of God." When you do what God wants you to do, your heart fills with God's presence and your strength inflates with God's blessing. Obedience leads to assurance of God's presence and joy in it. When you express your faith in God with obedience to God, you will know the glorious company of God at all times.

You will never regret obeying a God impulse.

85

When you ask me to do something for you, dear God, I am honored.

ॐAmen.

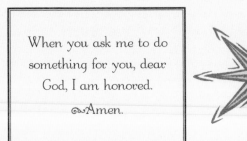

• • • • • • • •

🌿The Christmas Story

Where did the prophets say the Messiah would be born?

Matthew 2:4 NLT

In Bethlehem . . . for this is what the prophet wrote.

Matthew 2:5 NLT

Surely, from now on all generations will call me blessed.

Luke 1:48 NRSV

He has brought down the powerful from their thrones,
and lifted up the lowly; he has filled the hungry
with good things.

Luke 1:52–53 NRSV

My eyes have seen your salvation, which you have
prepared in the presence of all peoples.

Luke 2:30–31 NRSV

෨

• • • • • • •

The Gift of Christmas

We love you, Jesus. You're the best
God we ever had.

Nine-year-old boy

ಲ

In BC we know God is. In AD
we know who God is.

Author Unknown

ಲ

Reflecting on this birth, we recognize
the work of God embodied in it.

Martin Luther

ಲ

God is big enough—even for Christmas.

Handel H. Brown

ಲ

This Christ of Christmas shines down through
the ages like a gem with many facets.

Pam Whitley

ಲ

• • • • • • • •

Time to Wait

I will wait for the LORD, who is hiding his face
from the house of Jacob, and I will hope in him.

Isaiah 8:17 NRSV

❧

The four-week period before Christmas is called
Advent. The word advent derives from a Latin word that
means "coming." During the season of Advent, you wait
for the coming of God in Jesus at Bethlehem. You anticipate that moment when Mary looked for the first time
upon the face of her newborn baby. You strain your ears
toward the hills for a sound of angels singing. You look
for some shepherds who make their way to a cave so you
can go with them. You wonder where, in their arduous
journey, the Wise Men are by now. You search the skies
for a particularly bright star. And you wait.

You wait because you know what you wait for. You
wait because you know what you wait for is worth waiting for. An hour of waiting seems to take up most of the
day. It seems, at times, you have been put on permanent

• • • • • • • •

hold, but you know better. You know, at the end of the wait, there is Bethlehem. There are Mary and Joseph. You can see the shepherds looking up into the sky, the Wise Men on their camels trudging along. You can smell the hay in the manger. You can hear the angels tuning up.

You wait because you know, at the end of the wait, there is God.

Dear God, I wait for you to get to Bethlehem so you can come into my heart again.

Amen.

• • • • • • • •

Seek to Find

This will be a sign for you: you will find a child
wrapped in bands of cloth and lying in a manger.

Luke 2:12 NRSV

ᏇᏇ

There was a time in England, from 1558 until
1829, when certain people were not allowed to practice
their particular religion. It was during that time the
Christmas song "Partridge in a Pear Tree" was written as
a catechism song for young people. The song has two lev-
els of meaning, one obvious and one hidden. The hidden
meaning is religious in nature.

The partridge in a pear tree is Jesus Christ. The
two turtledoves are the Old Testament and the New
Testament. The three French horns stand for faith, hope,
and love. The four calling birds indicate the four Gospels
of Matthew, Mark, Luke, and John. The five golden rings
represent the Torah, the six geese a-laying stand for the
six days of creation, and the seven swans a-swimming are
the sevenfold gifts of the Holy Spirit. The eight maids

• • • • • • • •

a-milking are the eight beatitudes; the nine ladies dancing are the nine fruits of the Holy Spirit; and the ten lords a-leaping are the Ten Commandments. The eleven pipers stand for the eleven faithful disciples, and the twelve drummers symbolize the twelve points of belief in the Apostles' Creed.

Each element in the song stands for some great religious truth. Those who could not practice their faith openly were still able to hear the story.

God puts truth everywhere for you. It is in the Bible you read, the hymns you sing, the Christians you know. Seek, and you will find.

Dear God, praise your
holy name for the
many and creative
ways in which you
make yourself
known to me.
᷆Amen.

. . . .

The Star of Bethlehem

God sent a star to lead the Wise Men to the birth-place of baby Jesus where they gave gifts and worshiped. Their journey is beautifully captured in the carol "We Three Kings of Orient Are": "O star of wonder, star of night, star with royal beauty bright; westward leading, still proceeding, guide us to thy perfect light!"

Over the years, people speculated about the star. Some said it was Halley's comet; others said it was a nova that increased its brilliance hundreds of times. Some speculated it was a conjunction of Mars and Saturn. Whatever it was, God used the star to lead the Wise Men to Jesus.

Every Christmas, people across the world honor the star. In Bethlehem, Pennsylvania, citizens of the "Christmas City" have erected a huge electric star, symbolic of peace and goodwill. This great display, built on a

• • • • • • • •

steel structure nearly a hundred feet high, stands on a mountain, dominating the landscape and leading everyone to the truth of Christmas. Singers from the passion play in Oberammergau, Germany, go out to "follow the star" with a large star-shaped lantern. In Sweden, boys and girls wearing tall white hats trimmed with silver stars are led by a child with a large star, which has bells on each of its five points. In some countries, including Spain and Italy, people wait until the first star appears on Christmas Eve before beginning their celebration. Wise men and wise women still follow the star.

. . . .

Long Ago in Bethlehem

In the village of Bethlehem years ago lived a man who owned an inn where people stayed when they were traveling. His name was Mathan and his wife's name was Lycia. They had one child, an eight-year-old daughter called Susana. She helped her parents run the inn, cleaning the large room where people slept and stacking the pallets when the inn was not full. Mathan and Lycia were devout people who read the Scripture and followed God's law. They taught Susana to do the same.

> Joseph also went from the town of Nazareth in Galilee to Judea, to the city of David called Bethlehem.
>
> Luke 2:4 NRSV
>
> ᘐ

One evening, as light shone warmly from the window, Susana and her mother listened as Mathan read from God's Word. His voice filled the room as he read from the prophet Isaiah. "The Lord himself shall give you a sign; Behold, a virgin shall conceive, and bear a son, and

• • • • • • • •

shall call his name Immanuel" (Isaiah 7:14 KJV). Susana
loved this story and listened intently as her father continued reading. "Unto us a child is born, unto us a son is
given: and the government shall be upon his shoulder:
and his name shall be called . . . The Prince of Peace"
(Isaiah 9:6 KJV). Mathan finished reading, closed the book,
and they prepared to go to bed.

Just then a knock came at the door. Pilgrims had
been arriving for days to register for a government census,
and the inn was at capacity, but Mathan went to the door
anyway. He was considerate to everyone. Susana wondered who was at the door and where they would stay.
She went to the window and looked outside. "Oh, come,
Mother," she said to Lycia, "the woman is pregnant."

Lycia joined her at the window and looked out at a
woman about seventeen and a man some years older.
"Very pregnant," her mother added.

"Where will they stay?" Susana asked anxiously.

Her mother touched Susana's arm, smiled at her
daughter, and said, "Don't worry. Your father will figure
something out. He won't be able to turn them away. Not
with the woman pregnant."

CHRISTMAS IS . . .

• • • • • • •

Mathan did figure it out. He made a place for the couple out behind the inn in a cave he used as a stable. He put his donkey and three cows over in a corner of the cave and roped it off so this couple could use the rest of it for themselves and for their baby, who surely would be born soon. Mathan came back and the three of them went to bed.

Sometime during the night, Susana was awakened by a noise out behind the inn. It must be coming from the cave where the couple are staying, she thought to herself. She slipped from her bed and over to the window to peek out into the night. As she did, she heard the cries of a baby coming across the yard. "The young woman had her baby," Susana said aloud. As she looked out the window at the sky full of stars, she noticed one star much brighter than the others. In fact, it seemed the star had come to stand right over the cave where her father had housed the couple. In her heart, Susana knew something special was happening and ran out of the house and down to the cave. As she did, she saw men who looked like shepherds leaving the cave, talking excitedly among themselves. "What's going on?" Susana asked, and her question stopped them in their tracks.

• • • • • • • •

They looked at her, all of them smiling broadly, and said, "Messiah was born here tonight."

"Where? What do you mean?" Susana poured forth her questions.

The older of the shepherds replied, "The one Isaiah talked about. Immanuel."

"And Counselor and Mighty God," added another shepherd.

Susana's heart flooded with hope, and her cheeks flushed with joy. The Word of God her father had read that evening stirred in her heart, and she knew what the shepherds said must be true. The one the prophet had talked about had come. Right here in Bethlehem. Right here in her backyard.

Susana said a quick good-bye to the shepherds and ran toward the cave. As she got closer, she slowed her step and then stopped altogether. She approached a henna tree where creamy white, highly scented blossoms hung in clusters like grapes from a vine. She picked one of the clusters, held it tightly in her hand, and entered the cave. 🌿

• • • • • • •

🌿The Christmas Story

My servants will sing out of the joy of their hearts.

Isaiah 65:14 NIV

In that day the LORD Almighty will be a glorious crown,
a beautiful wreath for the remnant of his people.
He will be a spirit of justice.

Isaiah 28:5-6 NIV

This is how much God loved the world: He gave
his Son, his one and only Son.

John 3:16 THE MESSAGE

Joseph and Mary were amazed at what
was being said about Jesus.

Luke 2:33 NLT

At that moment she came, and began to
praise God and to speak about the child.

Luke 2:38 NRSV

෨

• • • • • • • •

The Gift of Christmas

The Christian church for the most
part does not ask the how of God
becoming a man but the why.

Madeleine L'Engle

∾

He created worlds and companied with
celestial beings, yet he came to live
in a family setting on earth.

Henry Gariepy

∾

The Christ-child lay on Mary's lap,
His hair was like a light.
(O weary, weary was the world,
But here is all aright.)

G. K. Chesterton

∾

In the little town of Bethlehem,
one silent night, the royal birth of
God's Son tiptoed quietly by.

Ken Gire

∾

The birth of Jesus is the sunrise of the Bible.

Henry Van Dyke

∾

. . . .

Set Ablaze

Were not our hearts burning within us while he talked with us on the road and opened the Scriptures to us?

Luke 24:32 NIV

ॐ

If you want to understand what happened at Christmas when God came to earth, get a piece of paper and a magnifying glass and find the sun at its highest in the sky. Place the piece of paper on the ground and the magnifying glass in your hand. Carefully position the magnifying glass between the sun and the paper. Then wait and watch. The sun's rays, enhanced and intensified by the magnifying glass, turn the paper a light brown and then a darker brown. After a while, the paper bursts into flame.

God put Jesus between heaven and earth at Christmas. In that position, Jesus magnifies God's love. The love that has been far away is now close up. It is warmer in intent and purpose than before. It comes to you precisely and directly. It warms your soul with its

• • • • • • • •

passion and dedication. It sets your heart ablaze in joy
and gratitude. God's love come down to earth in a
Bethlehem cradle takes the initiative and makes the first
step. God puts Jesus in position to come to you, ignite you
in the coming, and set your heart ablaze with the passion
of undeniable love.

God loves you first. God comes to you first.
God reaches down before you reach up.

> You are the God who comes.
> Thank you for coming to
> me in Jesus Christ.
> ⸎Amen.

• • • • • • • •

Where He Is Found

They entered the house where the child and his
mother, Mary, were, and they fell down before
him and worshiped him.

Matthew 2:11 NLT

ॐ

Henry van Dyke's The Story of the Other Wise
Man is a popular Christmas story about Artaban, who is
to meet his three friends and go in search of a new King.
He starts off with high hopes, carrying with him precious
jewels to give to the King when he is found. "Three great
gems—one blue as a fragment of the night sky, one red-
der than a ray of sunrise, and one as pure as the peak of a
snow mountain at twilight."

As he moves toward the meeting, he stops along the
way to help people who are in need. They are sick, hurt,
neglected. To each he gives one of his precious jewels,
which they are able to use to find relief and rescue.
Because of the delays this causes, Artaban misses the ren-
dezvous.

When Artaban gives away his last jewel, a radiant

• • • • • • • •

pearl, to a woman who has been seized for the debts of her father, he says, "This is your ransom. It is the last of my treasures I had for the King." It is then that Artaban, an old man now, finds the King he has sought. A voice wafts through the air, "Verily I say unto you, inasmuch as thou hast done it unto one of the least of these my brethren, ye have done it unto me."

Jesus is present in those you help. You never know when you will meet him.

Dear Jesus, I will look
for you more and
see you better.
ᏰᎪmen.

• • • • • • • •

The Christmas Story

At just the right time I will respond to you. On the day
of salvation, I will help you.

Isaiah 49:8 NLT

The Word was in the world, and . . . yet the
world did not recognize him.

John 1:10 GNT

He came to what was his own, and his
own people did not accept him.

John 1:11 NRSV

Some, however, did receive him and believed in him . . .
The Word became a human being and,
full of grace and truth, lived among us.

John 1:12, 14 GNT

To them He gave the right to become children of God.

John 1:12 NASB

☙

• • • • • • • •

The Gift of Christmas 🌿

Joseph places a garment beneath her, and
with a final push and a long sigh her labor
is over. The Messiah has arrived.

Ken Gire

☙

Every angel heard a faint redeeming
sound above the sleeping world. At the
very moment God dropped his hand,
they heard it. A baby cried!

Calvin Miller

☙

Christ was not half God and half man.
He was perfectly God and perfectly man.

James Stalker

☙

Jesus Christ is the condescension of divinity,
and the exaltation of humanity.

Phillips Brooks

☙

Jesus became as like us as God can be.

Donald English

☙

• • • • • • • •

Share the News

*Soon afterward Mary got ready and hurried off
to a town in the hill country of Judea. She went
into Zechariah's house and greeted Elizabeth.*

Luke 1:39-40 GNT

෩

106

The tree was decorated, presents arranged by
name under it, and the house glowed with signs of
Christmas. The everyday dishes had been put away, and a
full set of Christmas china was in the cabinet. The coffee-
mug rack was filled with cups painted with scenes of the
season. On every doorknob was a handmade cover featur-
ing a jolly Santa Claus. Stockings with sequined names on
them hung over the fireplace. Dishes were filled with
candy, and freshly baked pies scented their way through
the house.

Reggie and Oneita sat on the living room couch.
They were close together, holding hands. They were
waiting for their son and family to come from New
Mexico, their daughter and family from Michigan.
Preparations were complete. Only the people were miss-

• • • • • • •

ing. Later that day, when everyone had arrived, it was time to celebrate Christmas.

When an angel came to Mary and told her she would be the mother of God's Son, it was news too good to keep to herself. She trudged over hill and through valley until she got to the house of her aunt Elizabeth. It was a long and tiresome trip, but she stayed fresh by rehearsing to herself what she would say to Elizabeth. She had such good news to share.

Sharing is the art of giving from the heart. Christmas is meant to be shared.

107

Thank you, dear God, for news to share and people to share it with.
Amen.

. . . .

Treasure in a Feedbox

This is what you're to look for: a baby wrapped
in a blanket and lying in a manger.

Luke 2:12 THE MESSAGE

֍

The traditional folk tale The Tale of Three Trees
tells of three trees side by side on a mountain who know
what they want to be when they grow up. One tree wants
to be a mighty sailing ship that carries great kings across
mighty waters. Another wants to stay on the mountain,
grow tall, and give glory to God. The third tree dreams of
being a treasure chest covered with gold and filled with
priceless gems.

The tree that dreams of being a treasure chest covered with gold and filled with jewels is cut down and
taken to a woodcarver's shop. The tree thinks his dream
has come true. However, the tree is not made into a fancy
chest to hold diamonds and rubies; rather, it is made into
a crude box to hold feed for hungry animals. Many days
pass, and the tree has nearly forgotten the dream. But

• • • • • • • •

then, one night in a little town called Bethlehem, something happens to help him recall it. In a cave out behind a crowded inn, a young mother walks across a cold stone floor with a newborn baby in her arms and puts the baby in the feedbox made from his wood. That is the moment the tree is aware his dream has come true. He is holding the greatest treasure the world will ever know.

Christmas is holding the treasure of Jesus in your heart.

109

Come into my heart,
Lord Jesus. Come in
today. Come in to
stay. This I pray.
∽Amen.

· · · · · · · · ·

The Story of "Silent Night"

While the composition of Handel's Messiah and Bach's Christmas Oratorio in the eighteenth century brought the Christmas message to many, there was need for a simple song that could be sung by everyone. This was found in "Silent Night," whose words were written by a village priest and whose melody was composed by the church organist. Father Josef Mohr was pastor of a parish church in Austria, and Franz Gruber was the organist there.

In 1818, while Father Mohr was preparing the sermon for the Christmas service, he was asked to go out and bless a newborn baby. Perhaps seeing the child in his arms reminded him of Mary and her baby. When he got home, he rapidly wrote the words of what became the world's most popular Christmas carol. But he had no

• • • • • • • •

music for the words, and he wanted the composition sung at the Christmas service. So Father Mohr hurried over to see Franz Gruber, to ask him to furnish the melody for his words. Gruber, within an hour, completed the music and took the melody to Mohr. At the Christmas Eve service, the two men, singing tenor and bass, formed a quartet with two women singers. Unfortunately, mice had eaten at the organ bellows, and so, to the accompaniment of Father Mohr's Italian guitar, they introduced their composition to the world.

111

Like No Other King

His name was Argus, and he ruled a vast kingdom in the long ago. His kingdom stretched expansively for acres and miles across mountain, valley, and sea. The kingdom was called Argonia, and no country or nation rivaled it in size and resources. From its mountains came ores of great value, and from its seas and fields came food for many people. Its schools had no rivals, its artisans were world renowned, and its scholars had students everywhere. The music of Argonia was supreme, its poetry exquisite, its literature beyond comparison. The world had never known a kingdom like Argonia.

> Now to the King eternal, immortal, invisible, the only God, be honor and glory forever and ever. Amen.
>
> 1 Timothy 1:17 NASB

Over all of this Argus ruled, and he was a king with absolute control. People did what he said, exactly

112

• • • • • • •

how and when he wanted it done. He made all final decisions on every issue. No one overruled Argus, or even
thought of doing such a thing. His decrees were nonnego-
tiable, his laws absolute. He reigned over court and kingdom. He was never out of control, always in charge.

One time, King Argus was out visiting his subjects
from town to town. He was driven to the center of each
town in his golden carriage pulled by eight white horses.
Trumpets of high brass and great sound announced his
coming. He stepped onto the glorious red carpet that was
rolled out to the side of his carriage. He was covered in
flowing robes of glistening silk and was wearing his
crown of emeralds and pearls. Upon seeing him, his subjects bowed three times and shouted greetings of honor
and glory to the king. He was then taken to a high throne
from which he spoke to the people.

It was from such a throne in one of the towns near
the end of a day that he saw her. She was but a humble
maiden, but King Argus had never seen anyone so grace-
ful and so elegantly beautiful. None of the women at
court who adored him compared. No woman in the

• • • • • • • •

entourage of visiting dignitaries was half as beautiful. Her long, shining black hair cascaded down her back. Her green eyes sparkled. Her perfectly shaped face glowed. She was exquisite. And, as she stood in line to greet King Argus, she smiled at him. And his heart was never the same.

He discovered that her name was Capracia, and he decided he must have her as his own. But how would he do that? If he took her because he was king and could, she would not resist him. But would she ever love him? And she must love him as he loved her. Oh, she might say she loved him, for who would go against such a king? But would she really love him? It would not do to have her any other way. She must be truly happy at his side. She must genuinely love him. If he came back for her riding in his royal carriage with his armed escort waving the bright flags of the kingdom, that would no doubt overwhelm her. He wanted her to be his equal in love, not a cringing subject who grieved for the life she left behind.

As his longing increased and his heart ached, he finally decided what he would do. He left the palace one

• • • • • • • •

day without crown or chariot. There was no guard, no preceding fanfare. He was dressed in the plain brown garb of a commoner. He entered the village where Capracia lived, and no one recognized him. He went to the blacksmith's shop and there got a job making shoes for the horses of the hardworking farmers. He found a small room to rent and lived there by himself. He went to work each day, played with the children on the village green in the evening, and became a part of the community.

After several weeks, he presented himself to Capracia as one who had loved her from afar. He told her how she filled all the days of his heart and that, without her, he would be nothing. Over time, she came to love him as he loved her and they were married in the village church. It was only then he told her he was King Argus and that she would be his queen forever.

Christmas is when the King of kings walks into the village of your heart and you love him as he loves you. 🍂

• • • • • • • •

The Christmas Story

You, Bethlehem, David's country, the runt of the
litter—from you will come the leader who
will shepherd-rule Israel.

Micah 5:2 THE MESSAGE

"Behold, days are coming," declares the LORD,
"when I will make a new covenant with the house
of Israel and with the house of Judah."

Jeremiah 31:31 NASB

Nothing is impossible with God.

Luke 1:37 NLT

The LORD will still give you proof. A virgin is pregnant;
she will have a son and will name him Immanuel.

Isaiah 7:14 CEV

When the right time finally came,
God sent his own Son.

Galatians 4:4 GNT

. . . .

The Gift of Christmas

O God, you have proven your love for all
humanity by sending us Jesus Christ our Lord.

John Baillie

∽

There is in the world only one
figure of absolute beauty: Christ.

Fyodor Mikhailovich Dostoevsky

∽

Jesus Christ is the great name in history.

Pere Didon

∽

Christ's humanity is the great hem of the garment, through which we can touch his Godhead.

Richard Glover

∽

In Christ Jesus heaven meets earth
and earth ascends to heaven.

Henry Law

∽

Christmas, my child, is love in action.

Dale Evans Rogers

∽

• • • • • • • •

Part of the Family

From the Father his whole family in
heaven and on earth gets its name.

Ephesians 3:15 NIrV

෧෨

Robbie had graduated from college, got a job right away in his college town, and hadn't been home in almost three years. His dad and mom had been to see him four or five times, but due to his demanding work, he hadn't been able to get back to where he was born and raised.

Recently, Robbie had met the girl of his dreams and, after only two months, had asked her to marry him. This came as quite a shock to his folks. They had never met her, didn't know anything about her except what Robbie told them. Surely she was a fine young woman or Robbie would not have chosen her, but they didn't really have much to go on.

"Let's send Robbie airfare and get him home for Christmas," his dad said one evening.

• • • • • • • •

"He won't want to leave Charlotte," his wife replied.

"Well, that's easily solved," her husband said. "We'll send airfare for her, too."

The money had been sent, an invitation to visit warmly extended to Charlotte, and now Robbie and his fiancée walked into the house. They both stopped when they spotted a large and colorful banner hanging across the back wall of the living room: CHARLOTTE, WELCOME TO OUR FAMILY!

God's love for you at Christmas makes your family larger.

Dear God, thank you for everyone
you send to be part of my
family this Christmas.
Amen.

• • • • • • • •

Sing a Song

☙

It was Christmas Eve, and Kay's house was filled with family from many places across the country. Her aunt Lannie, a professional singer, had come from Minnesota. All the relatives were gathered around the piano in the living room singing Christmas carols.

During a lull in the singing, Kay asked her aunt, "What were you singing?"

Aunt Lannie responded, "I was singing alto."

Kay laughed as she responded, "Well then, no wonder you sounded funny. We were singing 'Joy to the World.'"

There is much joy to sing about at Christmas because "the Lord is come." God opened the door of heaven, and his only Son stepped across the threshold and over the stars to visit the earth as a precious little baby

· · · · · · · ·

nestled in a crib filled deep with straw and watched over by the most obedient people history has recorded. Years before, the prophet had said a child would be born and a Son would be given, and that's what happened. Mary's child was born, and God's Son was given. At Christmas, you sing joyfully of the one who is fully human and fully God. You lift your praise to God for the greatest event to ever take place. Jesus, in a loving act of downward mobility, is come to the world.

God is with you right now, and there is a feast of joy in your world.

121

Dear God, I fly the flag of
joy in my heart because
that is where you live.
☙Amen.

· · · · · · · ·

The Christmas Story

He was in the beginning with God.

John 1:2 NASB

The Spirit of the LORD will rest on him—the Spirit of
wisdom and understanding, the Spirit of counsel and
might, the Spirit of knowledge and the fear of the LORD.
He will delight in obeying the LORD.

Isaiah 11:2-3 NLT

In that day the wolf and the lamb will live together . . .
and a little child will lead them all.

Isaiah 11:6 NLT

We have seen his glory, the glory of the One and Only,
who came from the Father, full of grace and truth.

John 1:14 NIV

It's really happened! God has broken through to the
other nations, opened them up to Life!

Acts 11:18 THE MESSAGE

∾

• • • • • • • •

The Gift of Christmas

Christ is our temple, in whom
by faith all believers meet.

Matthew Henry

❧

The impression of Jesus which the Gospels
give . . . is not so much one of deity
reduced as of divine capacities restrained.

J. I. Packer

❧

He gave up all the glory of that world,
and was born of a poor woman.

Elijah P. Brown

❧

Behold how very ordinary and common things
are to us that transpire on earth, and yet how
high they are regarded in heaven.

Martin Luther

❧

Wherein our Savior's birth is celebrated,
the bird of dawning singeth all night long.

William Shakespeare

❧

• • • • • • •

It Happens Here

This was the first census that took place while
Quirinius was governor of Syria.

Luke 2:2 NIV

☙

When you read the Christmas story from the
Gospel of Luke, you might want to hurry on and get to
the part where choruses of heavenly beings carpet the
skies and sit on clouds, singing joyous stanzas of hope and
praise. But don't hurry on too quickly. Stop and linger
awhile around what seems to be a rather mundane inclu-
sion, that Quirinius was governor of Syria when Jesus was
born. That is more important than it appears to be.

The statement about who was governor of Syria
when Jesus was born fixes the coming of God to earth
along the continuum of history. God came not only in
human flesh but in human time. His coming was so liter-
al that now history is divided according to the years
before he came and the years after he came. Jesus Christ
split history right in two, and we know exactly when that

. . . .

happened. It happened when there was a woman named Mary and a man named Joseph who went to a place called Bethlehem. It happened when a census was taken in the land. It happened when Quirinius was governor of Syria.

The birth of Jesus happened then, and it happens now. It happened to them, and it happens to you.

125

Dear God, thank you
for your presence in
my history.
⁊Amen.

• • • • • • • •

Not Far to Bethlehem

*Does not the Scripture say that the Christ will
come from . . . Bethlehem?*

John 7:42 NIV

❧

In the children's book Probity Jones and the Fear
Not Angel by Walter Wangerin Jr., a young girl is sick and
cannot go to church to play the angel in the Christmas
pageant. The rest of her family leaves for church, and she
is at home alone. She looks out a window and sees a beautiful woman all dressed in white and looking right at
Probity. The woman smiles, opens the window, and tells
Probity it is time to go. "Go where?" Probity wants to
know, and the woman says, "Why, to the Christmas pageant, of course!" But it is not the Christmas pageant at the
church they go to. It is the first Christmas scene in the
long ago when Jesus was born in Bethlehem. The woman,
who is an angel, gathers Probity up in her arms, warms
the child with her breath, and soon they are flying over
city and country to a hillside where angels sing to shep-

• • • • • • • •

herds, and then the angel flies Probity to the door of a stable where she enters to kneel and worship the King of kings.

As an angel flies, it didn't seem Probity had to go far to get to Bethlehem. And neither do you. Bethlehem is wherever and whenever you celebrate the birth of Jesus Christ.

127

Dear God, thank you
for your birth in
my heart.
॰Amen.

. . . .

Christmas Gifts

When you understand what happened the first Christmas, you give gifts to others because of the gift God gives you in Jesus Christ. This puts you at the Bethlehem manger alongside the Wise Men, who brought gifts of gold, frankincense, and myrrh. Gold was a gift for a king. Frankincense was an ingredient in the oil used for religious anointing. Myrrh, a resin used at burials, was rare and costly.

The legend of Saint Nicholas, a bishop in the fourth century, is the next important segment of the Christmas gift-giving story. He went across Asia Minor giving gifts to poor children. Saint Nicholas's Day was the most exciting day of the year for thousands in Eastern and Central Europe. However, many European rulers ignored the example of Saint Nicholas and insisted they be given gifts

• • • • • • • •

by the common people. This practice was countered in the tenth century by King Wenceslaus, who roamed his kingdom during the holidays giving gifts to his subjects. During Martin Luther's time, people followed the examples of Saint Nicholas and King Wenceslaus and gave gifts anonymously to family, friends, and others. The practice of gift-giving at Christmas spread to the United States in the 1820s with the distribution of Clement Clarke Moore's poem The Night Before Christmas.

129

• • • • • • • •

What God Looks Like

 Hosef was one of the smartest people anyone had ever known. He could solve riddles, work puzzles, and prove theorems nobody else could. He had read all the great books, and written some of them himself. He was admired, honored, and revered. People came from far and near to ask him questions about many things, and Hosef always knew the answer.

> God himself was pleased to live fully in his Son.
>
> Colossians 1:19 CEV

Until one day a child came to see Hosef and bowed before the great scholar. "I have a question nobody's been able to answer," the child said. "They told me to come to you."

Hosef smiled and said, "What is your question?"

"What does God look like?" asked the child.

Hosef didn't have an answer to the child's question, and that question would send him wandering around the world. The great scholar vowed to find the answer to the

130

• • • • • • • •

question, no matter what it took. He canceled his many engagements, closed up his vast study, and set off with a few books, charts, and maps to find out what God looks like. He was not sure why the question had not previously occurred to him. It was fundamental and foundational, but Hosef had never considered that God looked like anything, or anybody. God is God, he had said and left it at that. But the child's question had burrowed deep into his curiosity. It haunted and hunted him, and he would not be satisfied until he had its answer.

He set off with a servant and provisions to make a long journey. He went to Mesopotamia, the land between two legendary rivers, and inquired of scholars he had previously met in his own country. They were intrigued by his question, but not one of them knew how to answer it. He went to Babylon and searched its vastness for someone who could help him. After all, it was the place of Hammurabi and his many and notable achievements, especially his magnificent code that had brought Babylon into its Golden Age. But even in Babylon, Hosef found no one who could answer the question that obsessed him. In Upper Mesopotamia, he went to Haran, which was located on a major east-west trade route that ran from the

CHRISTMAS IS . . .

. . . .

Tigris River on the east to the Mediterranean Sea on the
west. Surely someone there would have insight to share,
or at least could point him to a book or a map that would
shed light on the compelling question. Everyone tried.
Scholars studied to know, but no answer could be found.
He moved on to Ninevah, for he knew of its stature and
glory, and then to Nuzi, where there was an old scholar
who had discovered important tablets hidden deep in
the ground that told of ancient mysteries. Hosef pored
over them with the old man, but they discovered nothing
relevant.

Finally, in Jericho, the world's oldest city, Hosef
found someone to help him. A woman who studied the
heavens and found messages in the stars told him of a
particularly bright star she had seen recently that seemed
to be hovering over a little town southwest of Jericho.
Hosef's interest was aroused when the woman told him
the name of the town. He knew about Bethlehem. It was
David's city, and at least one prophet had predicted a special visitor from God would be born there.

With his servant, Hosef set out for Bethlehem in
late evening. They went only a short distance before it
was dark and the heavens filled with sparkling stars. As

• • • • • • •

the woman had said, one was brighter than all the others. "Let us go to where it is," Hosef told the servant. They did, and they went up a high hill and down into a valley with a limestone ridge lodged in its middle. The bright star stood over the ridge.

Hosef increased his walk to a half-run, leaving his servant behind, and saw a hole cut in the ridge. It was an entrance to a cave. The entrance was low, and Hosef bent over to look into the cave. Inside was a woman and a man keeping watch over a feedbox in which a newborn baby slept. Seeing Hosef peering into the cave, the woman smiled at him and said, "Welcome, stranger. Come join us, and see what God looks like." 🍂

. . . .

The Christmas Story

I will fulfill the good word which I have spoken
concerning the house of Israel and the house of Judah.

Jeremiah 33:14 NASB

The people who walked in darkness
have seen a great light.

Isaiah 9:2a GNT

They lived in a land of shadows,
but now light is shining on them.

Isaiah 9:2b GNT

Everyone in Jerusalem and Judah,
celebrate and shout with all your heart!

Zephaniah 3:14 CEV

In time to come you will acknowledge that
I am God and that I have spoken to you.

Isaiah 52:6 GNT

• • • • • • •

The Gift of Christmas 🎄

I sing the birth, was born tonight,
The Author both of life and light.

Ben Jonson

This is the month, and this the happy morn,
Of wedded maid and virgin mother born.

John Milton

The first Christmas was a simple
time of beauty and wonder.

Ace Collins

How silently, how silently,
the wondrous gift is given.

Phillips Brooks

Down in a lowly manger
The humble Christ was born,
And God sent us salvation,
That blessed Christmas morn.

Traditional

• • • • • • • •

Christmas Inspires

Mary said, "My heart praises the Lord;
my soul is glad because of God my Savior."

Luke 1:46–47 GNT

☙

Phillips Brooks was a highly successful pastor
and dedicated humanitarian. In the nineteenth century,
he joyfully and effectively proclaimed the gospel of Jesus
Christ. Not too many years after becoming a pastor,
Phillips Brooks made a pilgrimage to the Holy Land. He
saw many sights and talked to many people. He was there
riding on a horse from Jerusalem to Bethlehem on the
day before Christmas in 1865. He visited the field where
the shepherds heard the good news from angels, and he
was moved by the timelessness of the scene. As he
watched shepherds looking after their sheep, he knew it
was much the same as it had been that first Christmas. He
thought about God's great gift of love come to earth in
Jesus Christ.

Back in Philadelphia, Phillips Brooks wrote

• • • • • • • •

"O Little Town of Bethlehem" for his church. You have sung it many times. You will sing it this Christmas. When you do, remember the man who wrote it. Think about how he got in touch with the meaning of Christmas and, from that experience, created something beautiful for God and for God's people. His heart filled with God's love in Jesus Christ and overflowed into the majesty and glory of words that have blessed you many times, and will bless you again this Christmas.

Christmas fills the world with the music of love and hope.

Dear God, thank you for the
music and melody of Christmas.
∽Amen.

• • • • • • • •

Always Here

I am with you always.
Matthew 28:20 NIV

ॐ

Great people come into history. They achieve eminence, make an impact, and contribute their influence. Some formulate fresh ideas, others create new systems, and still others invent things never before thought of. They are noted, acclaimed, and applauded. Great people come into history, and then they leave.

Jesus Christ came into history. He came to the little town of Bethlehem, whose population was swollen by government edict. He found a place to be born where there was no place. Shepherds saluted him, astrologers worshiped him, Herod feared him, and angels heralded him. Jesus Christ came into history. Unlike others, however, he didn't leave. He stayed to love, bless, and heal. He remained, eternally the same, to illumine minds and change hearts. He lingered in the souls of women and

• • • • • • • •

men and whispered to them the secrets of God. He stayed
to build hospitals and erect schools, to raise churches
across the landscape, to inspire music and poetry, to give
counsel and provide direction to millions. He stayed to
stretch his hands across the centuries and control the des-
tinies of men, women, and nations. Jesus never leaves;
Jesus is always here. Jesus is nearer to you than you are to
yourself. Your life is held together by his presence.

Jesus comes again and again, is born over and over.
Every day is Christmas.

139

> Lord Jesus, thank you for
> coming to me every day
> in every way.
> ᕈAmen.

The Christmas Story

A child is born to us! A son is given to us!
And he will be our ruler.

Isaiah 9:6 GNT

The holy Child shall be called the Son of God . . .
And Mary said: "My soul exalts the Lord, and
my spirit has rejoiced in God my Savior."

Luke 1:35, 46–47 NASB

You . . . will name him Jesus—"God Saves"—
because he will save his people from their sins.

Matthew 1:21 THE MESSAGE

A little child shall lead them.

Isaiah 11:6 NRSV

Come . . . let us walk in the light of the LORD.

Isaiah 2:5 NIV

The Gift of Christmas

The world in solemn stillness lay
to hear the angels sing.

Edmund H. Sears

෮

Joy to the world! the Lord is come:
let earth receive her King.

Isaac Watts

෮

Welcome, all wonders in one sight!
Eternity shut in a span.

Richard Crashaw

෮

Our Christ is ever the Christ of abundances.

Clovis G. Chappell

෮

He became like you so that
you would come to him.

Max Lucado

෮